Romanian cookery

House of Guides PG

Project Manager: **Ioana Maria Radovici**

Photographer: **Tomoaki Minoda**
  www.dreamstime.com

Special thanks to **Mr. Teodor Meiță** and **MC MONI'S Restaurant**
(www.mcmonis.ro)

© House of Guides PG
Tel.: +40 212 243 183, +40 744 657 235; Fax: +40 212 243 186
E-mail: office@hogpg.ro
www.hogpg.ro

ISBN 978-606-8403-82-3

SUMMARY

Romanian culinary tour

*When I think about your extraordinary variety
of „Tchorba", what comes to my mind is not only
that people don't have a clue about Romania yet,
but also that you, Romanians, are far from knowing
your national wonders. In gastronomy, you are very,
very wealthy, in spite of your so-called poverty.*

Jacques Yves Cousteau

Beginning with Strabo, continuing with Tiberius Flavius, the Roman Ambassador who met king Decebal and dined with him in the year 106 A.D., joined then by Camille Julian, a French historian, who wrote of the Getic population, and further on by all the foreign travellers who visited the Romanian countries in the XIV-XIXth centuries, up to Romanian authors Negruzzi and Kogalniceanu, and to Pastorel Teodoreanu and Radu Anton Roman – not leaving out every major Romanian writer – despite of this extensive list we know too little about our fabulous cuisine.

As with the first editions this guide makes it its goal to highlight the main features of Romanian cuisine. To resort to a comparison with Romanian language, one could say we will only learn the basics of the vocabulary.

Barbarian cookery was based on smoke and salt, cabbage and onions, on millet broth and later on maize broth, on hot coal frying and garlic sauce.

The Romanian cuisine appointed as helpers hunting and fishing; it added also Turkish, Greek, Hungarian, Slavic (Russian, Polish, Ukrainian, Serbian) cooking notes, imported via the `48 Revolution Movement from Paris and Vienna. The friendly relationship with the Church led to some of the sweetest and easiest Lent food recipes.

Such a mix is hard to find anywhere else in the world. It resembles an attempt to combine living in a mountain cave with dwelling in a palace, or to blend a sun-scorched field and the Ducasse Salon in Monte Carlo. Well, all of this can be found in the unaffected and natural splendor of Romanian cuisine. What we are trying to do now is to write down for you all these recipes, to help you to discover their beauty, to prepare and enjoy them.

There is a single general true fact that applies throughout the history of our people, which has crossed such a troubled past, namely that Romanians have always enjoyed excellent meals.

Moreover, considering the fact that king Burebista failed in his attempt to completely burn down the vineyards in Dacia, despite the advice of his high priest, we will find out that, all along the history of the Romanian people, a glass of wine has always been present on the table. And since fiddlers used to be a customary company for the guests, there arises a refreshing picture of Romanian history. Nowadays, when the changes in the world are developing at top speed, there is only food preparation left to keep us humans in touch with nature's rate of life, which we should stay tuned to.

So, dear readers, we have the pleasure of inviting you to take a trip through this cook book and, with it, through yesterday's and today's Romania. However, there is one thing we ask you to do if you decide to sit down and eat: turn off your cell phone.

Appetizers, Snacks and Salads

In point of meal civilization (be it either lunch or dinner), the Romanian area has been, and still belongs to the Eastern world. There are long talking breaks between courses and the keynote of eating habits is generally a matter of greed and hurry, so that snacks are in fact often the main course. Let us remind the way guests use to ask the host what they will be served as appetizers, and then as main courses, so as to be prepared to size their appetite. It is said that in Romania one can gorge on snacks only: there are plenty of them, extremely savory and tasty. On the hors-d'oeuvre counter there is an abundance of every possible influence „poured" into Romanian cooking: Oriental, Slavic, Austrian, German or French. Mushroom stew in white sauce is of German origin – we, Romanians, added just more sour cream to it, pancakes Braşov Style come from Transylvanian Saxons (originally, German,

too), the same as are mushrooms with meat stuffing, potatoes with cheese and caraway filling, as well as baked beetroot with horseradish. Here is the Oriental influence, too: mashed white beans come from Turkish Bosforus, meat jelly from the Orient, broiled eggplant salad originated in Mediterranean cuisine (also Arabic, in the end), just as fried eggplants and green beans with garlic.

Roe salad is of Slavic descent, brought to Romania by Taras Bulba's Hahols, and baked bell peppers originate from Bulgaria, while under Turkish occupation.

Among all these appetizers, only one is of native Romanian descent: Dobrudja pie. It can be traced back to the times of Roman occupation, when sheep cheese and dough met the Roman baking pot. Then, the Roman pot was replaced by the Turkish tray, when Dobrudja fell under Ottoman occupation.

MASHED
WHITE BEANS

- **400 g white beans**
- **6 onions, sliced**
- **5-6 big garlic cloves, well crushed**
- **oil**
- **salt**

Soak dried beans in cold water for 5-6 hours or over the night. Boil beans 15-20 minutes in 4 l hot water with 1 teaspoon baking soda. Drain, then repeat two times the procedure without adding baking soda. Let beans boil in the „third water" until soften. Let boiled beans drain well until all water is gone and beans are lukewarm. Put beans in a blender, add salt and crushed garlic.
Blend and keep adding oil until the mixture becomes creamy and smooth.
Shallow fry half of the onion in a big frying pan. Stir continuously, so all onion slices become goldenbrown and crispy at one time. Drain on paper towel. Proceed in the same manner with the remaining onion. Serve well chilled bean mash with crispy fried onion.
Tip: don't over cook the beans – the mash will be watery. Add oil little by little, otherwise the mash may „curdle".

MUSHROOMS IN WHITE SAUCE

- **800 g fresh white mushrooms, diced**
- **200 g butter**
- **100 g white flour**
- **300 ml milk**
- **500 g sour cream**
- **2 tablespoons fresh chopped dill**
- **salt**
- **ground (white) pepper**

Simmer the mushrooms in 1 table-spoon of butter and ½ cup water. Begin to prepare a white sauce with flour, butter and milk. Boil it stirring continuously. Add sour cream and simmered mushrooms (with their boiling juice). Boil for another 5 minutes, and continue stirring. In the end, add the fresh dill. Serve it hot, with ground pepper.

Tip: this kind of creamy dish, based on white sauce, is called „ciulama". It can be also prepared with boiled chicken meat instead of mushrooms, some chicken broth instead of milk, without adding dill. It is delicious served with maize mash.

PANCAKE ROLLS WITH CHICKEN __ LIVERS AND MUSHROOMS __

FOR THE PANCAKES
- 3 eggs, beaten
- 400 ml milk
- 200 g wheat flour, sifted
- 1 tablespoon sunflower oil

FOR STUFFING
- 300 g chicken livers, diced
- 1 onion, finely chopped
- 200 mushrooms, finely sliced
- 2 eggs
- 1 teaspoon wheat flour
- 1/2 cup chopped fresh dill
- Salt, ground pepper

FOR FRYING
- 2 eggs, bread crumbs, flour

Prepare the pancakes. Beat eggs, oil, salt and flour with a mixer. Add milk, little by little, and keep beating. It must be a medium fluid batter, almost like a half-and-half. Pour 1.5-2 tablespoons of mixture in a well greased (buttered preferably) hot medium frying pan, spreading the mixture by a turning movement. When it becomes golden and thick, carefully turn the pancake on the other side, with a spatula.

Prepare stuffing. Stir-fry onion and mushrooms in hot oil (2 table-spoons), until the mushrooms juice evaporates. Add livers, and fry until it is medium done. Set aside. When lukewarm, add eggs, flour, dill, salt and pepper, and mix well.

Place 1-1.5 tablespoons of liver mixture on each pancake and roll the pancake, turning the ends inside. Roll each pancake-roll in flour, beaten eggs, and bread crumbs. Shallow fry in hot oil on all sides.

Tip: serve hot with sour cream and/or ketchup.

STUFFED
MUSHROOMS

- **1.2 kg big fresh mushrooms**
- **500 g minced pork**
- **2 tablespoons flour**
- **3 tablespoons boiled rice, well drained**
- **1 onion, finely chopped**
- **2 eggs**
- **100 g Swiss cheese**
- **1 tablespoon fresh chopped parsley**
- **salt, ground pepper**

Slice all mushroom stems. Stir-fry onion until it becomes transparent, and then add sliced mushroom stems and meat. Continue frying until meat is tender and the juice is evaporated. Let mixture get luke-warm, then mix with salt, pepper, flour, eggs, parsley and boiled rice. Spread a little salt and pepper on each mushroom cap, and then fill up mushrooms with the mixture. Set close together filled mushrooms on an oiled oven tray. Spread grated cheese on top of each mushroom. Bake until mushroom caps are tender and top cheese gets slightly brown. Serve warm.
Tip: you can serve the mushrooms with hot white sauce (béchamel) on top.

___CHICKEN MEAT JELLY___

- **1 kg breast and the wings from a farm raised chicken**
- **1 neck from a farm raised chicken (for its collagen content)**
- **1 onion, peeled**
- **1 carrot**
- **7-8 garlic cloves, smashed**
- **salt, pepper**
- **gelatine grains**

Set meat to boil into a pot, and pour enough cold water to top meat over for some 10 cm. Take off immediately all foam that is forming on the surface. Keep at medium fire. After 30 minutes, add salt and whole onion and carrot into the pot. Boil until meat separates almost itself from the bones and liquid is almost level with the meat. Set aside and allow cooling. When lukewarm, separate the meat (only breast and some of the wings), cut it into dices, and then place it in different bowls (you can decorate the bottoms with carrot dices, parsley, sweet corn grains, etc.). Blend smashed garlic into the soup, and strain the soup well. Distribute evenly the garlic flavored soup into the bowls. Cover bowls, and then place them in the fridge; when chilling, the soup must become a hard jelly. Serve very cold, directly from the bowl or overturned on a plate. It is very tasty sprinkled with (balsamic) vinegar, horseradish sauce or mustard.

Tip: test the soup's gelatine concentration by placing a small amount into the fridge; if it does not turn unto jelly, add some gelatine grains to the warm soup. For Christmas, it's traditionally made of pork meat (including ears, snout, legs).

MUSHROOMS
SCHNITZEL

- **18 medium white mushrooms**
- **3 eggs, beaten**
- **all-purpose flour**
- **bread crumbs**
- **salt**
- **ground pepper**

Wash the mushrooms well, cut level the legs. Spread with salt and pepper. Roll each mushroom first in flour, then in beaten egg, and finally in bread crumbs. Fry well on all sides in hot oil. Serve hot.

Tip: they are delicious as appetizer or as side dish with grilled beef.

FRIED EGGPLANTS
SALAD

- ▸ **6-8 long thin eggplants**
- ▸ **1 cup fresh chopped dill**
- ▸ **1 cup fresh chopped parsley**
- ▸ **8-10 garlic cloves, well crushed**
- ▸ **oil**
- ▸ **red vinegar**
- ▸ **salt**

Slice eggplants; the round slices must be no more than 1 cm thick. Spread salt on eggplant slices and let them drain for 20-30 minutes. Press the slices well in a paper towel to absorb juice and take out air from the texture. Shallow fry eggplant slices in hot oil until goldenbrown on both sides. Drain on paper towel. Serve cold with fresh parsley, dill, oil, red vinegar and garlic. Excellent as appetizer or side dish.

Tip: if eggplant slices are not well squeezed they will absorb a lot of oil when frying and will become greasy. Don't peel the eggplants – their fried skin is very tasty.

FISH EGGS DIP

- ▸ **3 tablespoons fresh water fish eggs (carp or pike)**
- ▸ **2-3 tablespoons lemon juice**
- ▸ **1 thick bread slice, without crust**
- ▸ **300 ml oil**
- ▸ **1 onion, finely chopped**
- ▸ **salt**

Soak bread in cold water, then squeeze it well in your hand. Smash bread well in a bowl with a fork, add lemon juice and onion. Begin adding oil and stir with the mixer, as you do when preparing a mayonnaise.
Don't add too much oil at a time because the dip will „curdle". Serve the dip on bread slices.
Tip: pike roe is the best choice. The dip must be a bit sour and very firm, harder than a mayo. You can also add some chopped chives or green baby onion.

BROILED EGGPLANT
SALAD

- **2 kg round and mature eggplants**
- **2 small onions, finely chopped**
- **150-200 ml oil**
- **salt**

Broil the eggplants directly on the fire. Turn them on all sides. Put aside on a tray to cool and drain. Cut the base of the stalk, and then cut each eggplant lengthwise. Take off the pulp with a tablespoon and put it in a plastic strainer. When all the juice is well drained, put the eggplant pulp on a wooden board. Chop the pulp finely with a knife (preferably a wooden one). Put the pulp in bowl, add onion and salt. Beat well with a fork or a mixer and add oil in small quantities until the eggplant salad becomes very creamy. Serve it well chilled on a platter or in tomato „shells" with bread and fresh tomatoes. It is also delicious with broiled bell pepper salad.

Tip: this creamy salad is, in fact, a kind of dip. You can add egg yolk and/or sour cream, diminishing the quantity of oil. It goes well with a glass of tzuica or palinca.

DOBRUDJA CHEESE PIE

- ▸ **600 g pastry dough**
- ▸ **500-600 g sheep feta cheese**
- ▸ **2 eggs**
- ▸ **3 tablespoons heavy sour cream**

Cover the oiled bottom of a round oven tray with ½ of the dough. Mix cheese, eggs and sour cream well. Spread cheese mixture in the tray, then cover with remaining dough. Prick the surface of the pie with a fork. Bake in preheated oven until goldenbrown. Serve warm or cold with yogurt.

Tip: the traditional Dobrudja recipe uses home made dough and a special cheese kept rapped in sheep stomach.

GREEN BEANS
SALAD

- ▸ **1.2 kg green beans**
- ▸ **1 cup fresh chopped dill**
- ▸ **1 cup fresh chopped parsley**
- ▸ **2 tablespoons well crushed garlic**
- ▸ **salt**
- ▸ **oil**
- ▸ **red vinegar**

Boil green beans in hot water for 10-12 minutes. Drain and let cool off. Make sauce by mixing salt, garlic, oil, and red vinegar. Pour sauce over chilled beans. Spread parsley and dill, then serve as salad or as side dish.

Tip: don't set to boil green beans in cold water – they will harden.

RED BEET ROOT
SALAD

- **1 big beet root (1.5 kg)**
- **2 tablespoon finely grated horseradish**
- **oil**
- **salt**
- **vinegar**

Preheat oven. Wash the beet root thoroughly and place it in the hot oven. Bake at moderate temperature until tender, rolling it from one side to another. When well done, the fork can easily enter the middle of the beet root. Let it cool, and then peel it with a sharp knife. Slice the beet root; add oil, vinegar and salt. Serve it cold as salad with grated horseradish or horseradish cream. **Tip:** use only mature beet roots with very dark purple color; scratch the skin a little with your nail to see if the inside of the root has the good color. It can be baked faster in the microwave oven at maximum temperature.

BROILED BELL
PEPPERS SALAD

- **2 kg bell peppers**
- **oil**
- **salt**
- **vinegar**

Place a thin iron sheet directly on the fire. Broil peppers on all sides. Put them immediately in a covered pan, spread some salt, and let them cool slowly. Carefully, peel the peppers, place them on a salad plate, spread salt, oil and red vinegar. Serve cold, as salad or side dish.

Tip: use long red sweet pepper; they are very easy to peel. You can add some crushed garlic in the sauce.

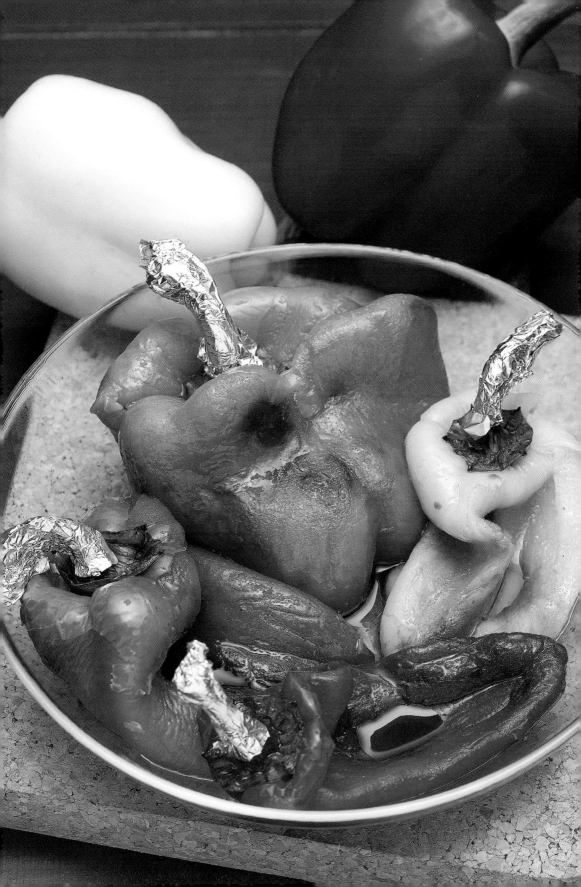

Soups and Tchorba

We, Romanians, enjoy the benefits of a unique gastronomically blend: we have taken over the vegetable soups and added further influences to them: meat balls from the Turks, lettuce from the Austrians, dry beans with smoked meat from the Germans (via Polish mediation). We added pork meat to our sour soups during the Turkish reign, because they had taken away our cattle as tribute, and then, during the Austrian rule, in Transylvania, we added tarragon (this is a German cooking habit). We prepared lamb borscht locally, as we used to be shepherds. Lentil soup is an Arabian import (in fact, lentils proper), that came to us also through the Turks. The other notes and shades - oil, vinegar, sour cream, borscht itself, depend on regional gastronomy use and practice.

MEAT BALLS
TCHORBA

- **400 g veal marrow bones**
- **300 g minced beef**
- **1 l wheat borsh**
- **2 tablespoons rice**
- **1 carrot, coarsely grated**
- **1 parsnip, coarsely grated**
- **1 cup celery leaves, chopped**
- **2 onions, finely chopped**
- **1 bell pepper, chopped**
- **1 big tomato, coarsely cut**
- **1 cup fresh chopped lovage leaves**
- **1 cup fresh chopped dill**
- **1 cup fresh chopped parsley**
- **salt**
- **pepper**

Boil bones in salted water for about one hour together with celery leaves and one chopped onion, and then remove bones from pot. Mix meat with remaining onion, rice, half of dill and parsley, salt and pepper. Mold mixture into balls and introduce them into the boiling bone soup. Add remaining vegetables into the soup. Boil for about 30-40 minutes. When the meat is tender, add borsh and let them boil for another 1-2 minutes. Finally, sprinkle with lovage, remaining dill and parsley. Serve hot. You can also add sour cream when serving.

Tip: lovage is a must when using borsh. Never boil borsh more than 1-2 minutes – long boiling time will ruin its special flavor.

LETTUCE AND BUTTERMILK SOUP

- **2 lettuces, coarsely chopped**
- **1 big onion, chopped**
- **1 big carrot, coarsely grated**
- **100 g smoked bacon, finely diced**
- **1 teaspoon wheat flour**
- **1 l buttermilk**
- **salt, vinegar**

Stir-fry bacon in a pot with some oil, until slightly golden; then add onion and carrot. Continue stir-frying until onion becomes transparent. Add salt and no more than 2 cups hot water. Let boil for 5 minutes, then add lettuce and let boil for another 5 minutes. Dilute flour in some cold water, and then blend in the buttermilk little by little. Pour buttermilk into the soup and boil for 2-3 more minutes. Serve hot with some vinegar drops.

Tip: you can serve after adding diced simple omelette into the soup. You can replace buttermilk with 700-750 g plain yogurt, but you must add one more cup of water.

Soups and Tchorba

WHITE BEANS AND SMOKED BACON SOUP

- **350 g dried white beans**
- **150 g smoked bacon, diced**
- **1 big onion, finely chopped**
- **1 carrot, diced**
- **1 bell pepper, chopped**
- **2 tomatoes, chopped**
- **2 tablespoons oil**
- **1 tablespoon tomato paste**
- **1/2 teaspoon dry thyme**
- **1/2 teaspoon dry dill seeds**
- **1/2 cup fresh chopped parsley**
- **1/2 cup fresh chopped dill**
- **salt**

Soak dried beans in cold water for 5-6 hours or over the night. Boil beans 15-20 minutes in 4 l hot water with 1 teaspoon baking soda. Drain, and then repeat the procedure without adding baking soda. Drain again.

Meanwhile fry onion, carrot, bell pepper and bacon in hot oil, in a pot, until onion becomes transparent. Add beans, tomatoes, pepper, salt, thyme, dill seeds, and 1.5 l hot water. Let it boil. When beans are ready, add tomato paste, stir, and boil for no more than 5 minutes. Serve hot with parsley and dill.

Tip: serve with lettuce salad and onion. You can also add fresh chopped tarragon and some vinegar drops.

PORK TCHORBA WITH TARRAGON

- **400 g diced pork meat**
- **4-5 pork spare ribs**
- **1 carrot, coarsely grated**
- **1 onion, chopped**
- **1 small parsnip, coarsely grated**
- **2 tablespoons celery root, coarsely grated**
- **2 tablespoons fresh chopped tarragon**
- **2 tablespoons rice**
- **1 egg**

Put meat and ribs in 3 liters of cold water, in a deep pot. Add some salt. Boil for about 1 h and take off immediately all foam that is forming on top of the liquid. When meat is almost done, add vegetables and rice. When finishing the boiling, add tarragon and remove it from the fire. Beat egg with sour cream. Serve hot with sour cream and vinegar.

Tip: you can use smoked spare ribs, and replace rice with one cup of diced peeled potatoes. Vinegar is a must.

LAMB BORSH

- **600 g lamb meat (neck and loin)**
- **1 small onion, chopped**
- **8-10 stalks baby green onion, coarsely chopped**
- **1 carrot, coarsely grated or diced**
- **1 liter wheat borsh**
- **1 cup fresh chopped lovage leaves and stalks**
- **1 egg, beaten**
- **2 tablespoons rice, washed and drained**
- **Salt**

Wash and coarsely cut the lamb meat (with bones). Set to boil in 2 l cold salted water; take off immediately all foam that is forming on top of the liquid while boiling. When meat is almost done, add vegetables and rice. Boil until meat and rice are done. Add wheat borsh, then boil for no more than 1-2 minutes. Blend egg with some cold water and 1 cup tchorba, added little by little. Pour egg mixture into the hot tchorba immediately and stir well. Serve with lot of chopped lovage.

Tip: it's a traditional Easter dish. Do not add any other vegetables besides onion and carrot. If the wheat borsh is not sour enough, you can add some lemon juice. The lovage is an absolutely must.

LENTILS SOUP

- **300 g lentils**
- **1 carrot, coarsely grated**
- **1 big onion, finely chopped**
- **1 teaspoon thyme**
- **3-4 garlic cloves, finely diced**
- **salt**
- **oil**
- **vinegar**

Put lentils and onion to boil in a deep pot, with 5 cups of cold water. When lentils almost done, add carrot, cloves and thyme. Serve well warm, adding salt, oil and vinegar into the dish.

Tip: never add salt before the lentils are well boiled – they may harden. This soup is tastier served with lettuce salad and green baby onions.

Main Courses

Here, too, we can witness the same show. Romanian meals are subject to plenty odd influences. Our selection focuses mainly on the Oriental origins of Romanian cooking. Meatballs, meat rolls in cabbage leaves, „mititei" (small, grilled forcemeat sausages), moussaka and vegetables ragout, al of them being the legacy we have received from Turks, Greeks or Bulgarians from the area of Arabian cooking. Vegetables stuffed with meat date back to the times of Turkish ruling in Dobrudja; a special route has been that of themoussaka, that returned to Romania after the Macedo-Romanians were forced by the Greeks to return to their native country. It was then that they brought back the moussaka, which had fallen back into oblivion during the Ottoman rule.

Certainly, all these different dishes show local influences too (tarragon, sour cream, cabbage, vine leaves etc).

Lamb haggis and onion and garlic stew are two dishes coming from the depth of Romanian history (both of them are prepared with lamb meat!), but they have been altered by later Oriental influences.

We can ascertain an Austrian import, too, originating – actually – in French cooking: this dish is chicken with sour cream from Bucovina, that stressed its local origins by simply replacing the French white sauce with plain Bucovina sour cream. The mushroom schnitzel from Banat has a somewhat peculiar story, it was brought here by Maria Theresa along with the Swabian settlers. In those days, the Banat province still had forests.

Nowadays, this special dish is more or less what's left to it!

An ancient Moldavian dish is fish in cheese casing, a preparation that joins the ancient shepherds and fishermen, marked by the superposition of the contribution of the Kiev Principality – i.e., it came once again from the Slavs, but it is impregnated by the taste delights of the noblemen on the shores of the Dniester. The fish cooked as „plachia" is also of Slavic origin, but it got refined by addition of bell pepper coming from the Bulgarians immigrants to the principalities. The butcher's stew can be dated sometime in the 18th century, as proven by its name, too – when the first butcher's shops appeared, there was not only meat for sale, but also prepared food.

The only genuine Dacian dish in this range is the „bulz" (polenta chunk with cheese) from the Maramureş, which has its own special story: in ancient times, in the days of our ancestors, this dish used to be made of millet and was cooked in live brand, just as it is nowadays. When the Turks took our cereals as a tribute, the Romanians learned to eat „cucuruz" (as maize was called originally, when it arrived in this area under the name of „granturco", bought from the Genovese merchants). That's where polenta originates and while neither wheat nor millet were available, cheese began to be wrapped in a chunk of corn flour. Originally, similarly to present Maramureş practice, it was cooked on live brand and did not contain any butter or sour cream, just cheese in skin bag, and nothing else.

GRILLED MEAT BALLS (MICI)

- **1.2 kg mixed ground meat (pork, lamb and beef)**
- **1 tablespoon baking soda**
- **2 tablespoons salt**
- **1 tablespoon ground pepper**
- **1/2 tablespoon ground cumin**
- **1 tablespoon dried thyme**
- **10-12 garlic cloves, crushed**
- **1/4 cup beef stock**

Mix all the ingredients together well. Leave mixture in the fridge to set for a couple of hours or ideally overnight – this is an important step that aids the meat in coming out tender.

Form into little 10-12 cm long sausage shapes. Grill on very hot grill, turn once. Serve hot mustard and salads.

Tip: put some water in a bowl to wet your hands when forming the sausages (this prevents the meat from sticking on your fingers). To get this right, if you have access to a butcher, ask the butcher to double grind the meat and to add some pork fat in the mixture - this melts off while grilling, but keeps the meat rolls moist and tender.

BEAN STEW WITH SMOKED BACON

- ▸ **500 g dried beans**
- ▸ **200 g smoked bacon, diced**
- ▸ **2 onions, finely chopped**
- ▸ **1 carrot, diced**
- ▸ **2 bay leaves**
- ▸ **3 tablespoons oil**
- ▸ **1 teaspoon whole black pepper**
- ▸ **1 tablespoon tomato paste**
- ▸ **1/2 teaspoon dry thyme**
- ▸ **salt**

Soak dried beans in cold water for 5-6 hours or over the night. Boil beans 15-20 minutes in 4 l hot water with 1 teaspoon baking soda. Drain, then repeat the procedure without adding baking soda. Drain again. Meanwhile fry onion and bacon in hot oil, in a pan, until onion becomes transparent. Add drained beans, carrot, bay leaves, pepper, salt, thyme, and enough hot water to cover well the beans. Let it boil covered, stirring gently from time to time. If the sauce becomes too thick before the beans are soft, add some water. When beans are ready, add tomato paste, stir very gently, and boil for no more than 5 minutes. Serve hot with fried smoked sausages, lettuce salad and onion. **Tip:** use a pan with thick bottom. Don't add too much water from the beginning because the sauce will be in excess and too thin. The baking soda is used to reduce the stomach discomfort.

BUTCHER'S STEW

- ▸ **200 g pork, diced**
- ▸ **200 g beef, diced**
- ▸ **50 g smoked bacon, diced**
- ▸ **100 g smoked sausages, diced**
- ▸ **500 g peeled potatoes, sliced**
- ▸ **60 ml oil**
- ▸ **1 tablespoon tomato paste**
- ▸ **1 cup chopped onion**
- ▸ **50 ml white wine**
- ▸ **4-5 garlic cloves, chopped**
- ▸ **1 cup fresh chopped parsley**
- ▸ **salt**
- ▸ **ground pepper**
- ▸ **thyme**

Sprinkle meat with salt, then stir-fry in hot oil with a little water. Add onion, garlic, smoked bacon and sausages; let them fry a little together, under constant stirring. When onion gets almost golden, add tomato paste, salt, pepper and thyme. Add warm water to cover ingredients, cover the pot and leave on medium heat for about one hour. Meanwhile boil potatoes in salted hot water. When the stew is ready, add wine, stir and remove from stove. Served with hot potatoes, sprinkled with parsley.
Tip: delicious also with maize mash and broiled bell pepper salad as side dish. Serve with a glass of Palinca or Horinca.

BAKED MAIZE MASH BALLS

- **400 g ground maize (maize flour)**
- **1.6 l milk**
- **300 g sheep feta cheese**
- **200 g butter**
- **salt**

Mix well maize, milk and some salt, in a thick bottom pot. Set to boil and stir continuously. When bubbling, continue boiling and stirring for another 10 minutes. Tipple maize mash over a wooden board; wait until it chills and hardens. Form mash balls with your hands. Mix cheese with half of the butter. Stuff the inside of the mash balls with some cheese mixture, and grease the surface of the mash balls with butter. Set on buttered oven tray and bake for about 10 minutes until lightly golden. Serve hot with onion and sour cream.

Tip: you can add inside the balls a hard boiled egg, shells off.

___ STUFFED VEGETABLES ___

- ▸ **400 g minced meat mix (pork and beef)**
- ▸ **2 big onions, chopped**
- ▸ **2 teaspoons rice**
- ▸ **1 cup fresh chopped parsley**
- ▸ **1 cup fresh chopped dill**
- ▸ **2 medium tomatoes**
- ▸ **1 medium eggplant**
- ▸ **1 whole bell pepper**
- ▸ **1 bell pepper, chopped**
- ▸ **1 marrow squash (courgette) peeled**
- ▸ **salt**
- ▸ **ground pepper**

Mix together meat, washed and drained rice, 2 tablespoons chopped onion, 1 tablespoon dill, 1 tablespoon parsley, salt, and ground pepper. Peel the marrow. Fry the eggplant a little in hot oil, on all sides. Cut in two the marrow and the eggplant. Hollow out partially the inside of the eggplant, marrow, and one tomato; put aside the pulp. Take off the seeds of the bell pepper. Coarsely chop the remaining tomato as well as the pulp of the marrow and eggplant. Prepare the sauce. Stir-fry in a medium deep pan the remaining chopped onion with 3 tablespoons oil until onion becomes transparent. Then add chopped bell peeper and vegetable pulp. Continue stir-frying for 10 minutes.

Stuff bell pepper, tomato, eggplant, and marrow pieces with the meat mixture. Place the stuffed vegetables close together in the pan, over the sauce, with their "mouths" up. Pour some warm water, enough to almost cover the top of the vegetables. Place pan in hot oven and bake for one hour, or until meat is tender and sauce becomes thick. Spread chopped dill and parsley, and then serve.

Tip: delicious served with sour cream or yogurt. You can place inside each eggplant one small garlic clove. The dish can also be prepared with only one kind of vegetables: only bell peppers, tomatoes, marrow or eggplants, but it is tastier when all flavors combine.

LAMB STEW WITH GREEN
_ BABY ONIONS AND GARLIC _

- **1 kg lamb meat, diced**
- **1 chopped onion**
- **1 tablespoon flour**
- **1 cup fresh chopped dill**
- **150 ml oil**
- **20-30 green baby onion stalks**
- **20-30 green baby garlic stalks**
- **1 tablespoon tomato paste**
- **1-2 tablespoons red vinegar**
- **salt**
- **ground pepper**

Cut green baby onion and garlic in pieces about 10-12 cm long; stir them fry in a pan with hot oil, until just tender, then remove from pan and drain. In the same oil stir-fry meat and chopped onion, with salt and some ground pepper, until meat is light brown and onion is transparent. Add to pan warm water to almost cover meat; cook covered, on low heat, until the meat is cooked through. Mix flour with a little cold water, vinegar and tomato paste, and pour this sauce over the meat in the pan. Add green onion and garlic pieces, stir gently to blend, and let it cook for 5 more minutes. Serve hot sprinkled with chopped dill.

Tip: for a special look, you can stir-fry greed baby onions and garlic without cutting them. Remove from pan when soft, let drain a little, then make a bow of each stalk. For the rest, you proceed the same.

SOUR CABBAGE ROLLS

- ▸ **1 medium brine pickled cabbage (sauerkraut)**
- ▸ **250 g minced pork**
- ▸ **250 g minced beef**
- ▸ **200 g smoked bacon**
- ▸ **300 g smoked spare ribs**
- ▸ **1 cup tomato juice**
- ▸ **250 ml dry white wine**
- ▸ **2 teaspoons dry thyme**
- ▸ **2 teaspoons dry dill seeds**
- ▸ **2 teaspoons whole black pepper**
- ▸ **2 teaspoons rice, washed**
- ▸ **ground black pepper**

Separate and wash the cabbage leaves in warm water if they are too salty; cut the thick base of the stalks. Depending on its size, cut each leaf in 2-4 parts, no bigger than your hand. Mix well meats, onion, rice, some ground pepper, and 1/2 teaspoon thyme. Add only a small amount of salt. Place 2 teaspoons of meat mixture on each cabbage piece, and then roll. Push inside with your finger the ends of each roll, to prevent meat getting out. Finely chop the remaining cabbage leaves. Cover the bottom of a pan with some of the chopped cabbage, the smoked spare ribs, whole black pepper, and dill seeds. Put cabbage rolls close together in the pan, spread thyme and slices of smoked bacon between them. Cover with chopped cabbage. Pour the tomato juice, the wine and enough water to cover well the cabbage. Bake in preheated oven until tender and slightly brown.

Tip: use a Roman covered clay pot instead of usual pan – it keeps all flavors. Serve it with fresh hot chilly peppers and maize mash. It goes also well served with some sour cream on top.

MEATBALLS WITH TARRAGON AND SOUR CREAM SAUCE

- ▸ **400 g minced beef**
- ▸ **200 g minced pork**
- ▸ **1 tablespoon wheat flour**
- ▸ **1 medium potato, peeled and finely grated**
- ▸ **2 eggs**
- ▸ **1 small onion, finely chopped**
- ▸ **400 g sour cream**
- ▸ **2 tablespoons fresh chopped tarragon**
- ▸ **2 tablespoons fresh chopped dill and parsley**
- ▸ **salt**
- ▸ **ground black pepper**

Mix well together meats, onion, parsley, dill, potato, eggs, salt and pepper. Make small round meatballs and roll them in flour. Put meatballs in an oiled oven tray and pour sour cream all over them. Bake in hot oven until meatballs are tender. Spread tarragon and serve hot with lettuce salad.

Tip: when using dry tarragon, put half of the quantity and add it few minutes before taking the tray out of the oven.

VINE
LEAVES ROLLS

- **200 g minced pork**
- **200 g minced beef**
- **young vine leaves**
- **1 tablespoon rice**
- **2 chopped onions**
- **200 ml oil**
- **1 tablespoon tomato paste**
- **1 teaspoon flour**
- **1 cup fresh chopped dill**
- **1 cup fresh chopped parsley**
- **salt**
- **pepper**

Choose medium-sized vine leaves, not large ones, as they are too old and hard to cook. Cut off the stalks of the leaves, which are then soaked shortly in salted boiling water. Blend meat with 1/2 of the chopped onion, rice, 1/2 of the dill and parsley, salt and pepper to taste. Place some of the meat mix on each vine leaf, close the leaves into rolls and place them in a pan. Cook the remaining onion in some hot oil, add the tomato paste, the flour mixed with a little cold water, and pour the resulting sauce over the meat rolls. Add water to cover the rolls and cook in oven at medium heat for one hour, until sauce is reduced and thickened. Sprinkle with the remaining dill and parsley.
Serve hot.
Tip: excellent served with sour cream or yogurt. Dill is a must.

SOUR CREAM TROUT

- 6 medium size trout fillet
- 5 tablespoons flour
- 6 tablespoons oil
- 2 small onions
- 1 garlic clove
- 200 ml cream
- 3 tablespoons butter
- salt
- pepper
- parsley

Gut and clean the fish thoroughly. Wash several times changing the water after each time so as to make sure you have the cleanest ingredient possible, than dry each fish.

Use all the salt and paper your taste buds can take to season the trout both inside and out.

After that you get to wallow it on a plate containing 4 of the tablespoons of flower. Make sure you have them all nicely covered.

Use a high frying pan to heat up the oil before placing the trout in. The frying process should be quick and the high oil temperature will give you the best, crispy on the outside soft on the inside, trout. After you have completed the process, just try to keep the worm while you prepare the sauce.

Chop the onions and cook them in butter over mild fire. As you do that, mix 250 ml of water with flower and incorporate the resulted product into the sourer cram. Then put the entire mix into the pan alongside the undercooked onions. Add garlic and season with pepper and salt. You could use wine instead of water but you are best to stay away from the stronger sentiments as they tend to lend too much of their flavor.

To top it all of, take the trout and fit it in the pan along side the sauce, add the parsley and let it cook for another few minutes.

EASTER LAMB TERRINE

- **1.5 kg lamb viscera (liver, lungs, kidneys and heart)**
- **15 green baby garlic stalks, chopped**
- **15 green baby onion stalks, chopped**
- **1 cup fresh chopped parsley**
- **1 cup fresh chopped dill**
- **2 hard boiled eggs, coarsely chopped**
- **3 large eggs**
- **1 big white onion, chopped**
- **1 lamb peritoneum for rapping**
- **butter for frying**
- **salt, ground pepper**

Set lamb organs to boil in cold water. When they are soft, set aside to cool. Stir-fry white onion in some butter, until soft and slightly golden. Chop the boiled organs, and then blend them with all other ingredients. Rap the mixture into a piece of lamb peritoneum (thoroughly washed), oil the surface, and then place the lamb terrine into an oiled casserole. Bake in medium hot oven until well baked inside. Serve hot or cold, with lettuce salad.
Tip: is a spring dish, blending spring flavors, thus you really need important amounts of green fresh stuff (garlic, onion etc.).

BAKED FISH DISH

- **1.2 kg carp filets**
- **3-4 big onions, sliced**
- **500 g fresh tomatoes, sliced**
- **3 bell or mild peppers, sliced**
- **1 bay leaf**
- **5-6 garlic cloves, sliced**
- **200 ml oil**
- **1 tablespoon tomato paste**
- **150 ml dry white wine**
- **ground black pepper**

Fry onion, bell peppers and bay in hot oil for 5 minutes, stirring occasionally, until onion becomes transparent or slightly golden. Add tomatoes, tomato paste, garlic and wine. Simmer for about 15 minutes. Add salt and ground pepper.

Put the fish filets in an oven tray, cover with the vegetable stew, and bake for 20 minutes.

Tip: ideal prepared with carp, but you can use any big fresh water fish filets. It can be served warm or cold, with a glass of good dry white wine.

Sweets

Native Romanian desserts are many and savory. Due to one and the same reason: the meeting between Oriental cooking (probably the most devillish, when it comes to sweets) and French cuisine, brought by the Frenchified youth to the Romanian Principalities in the mid-19th century, and also with Austrian cookery (a particular blend of relatively poor Anglo-Saxon influences with the same Oriental, Italian and French cooking).
You surely understand the result of such historically repeated influences, exposed to mutual corrections.
Our selection comprises a wide range of preparations: Oriental cheese dumplings (arrived with the Phanariots), Moldavian „holly eights" (small knot-shaped cakes prepared especially for the Forty Martyrs day and which arrived quite late on Romanian territory as a local religious graf ton Slavic influence), Moldavian sweet bread with raisins (which, as much as it may make you smile, has come to us from Italy, via the „official" cuisine of the Austrian-Hungarian Empire), jam pancakes (that, as far as I can remember, are to be found in 200 investigated food recipes, cakes and other household matters, written by Kogălniceanu and Negruzzi and published in 1841 – unmistakebly, French influence), as well as the Romanian cream cheese Easter cake (a native preparation, born in the times of the „great mumbling", when the current language in the Orthodox Church used to be Slavonic and the churchgoers couldn´t understand a word – a flokloric religious product, originated out of Christian images). Last, but not least, there is the traditional „coliva" (a kind of funeral porridge), which some people attribute to the the Serbian populations of the Balkans. However, this is a dish as such, an everyday dessert with historical roots, since the very times of Thracians and Dacians. In his writings, Strabon describes a lunch meeting (a banquet) between Aurelius, Trajan´s ambassador and Decebal, in the period when the Roman emperor wanted to obtain the rule over Dacia without a battle. During that meal, Aurelius was served with funeral porridge made of crushed millet, honey and walnuts. The Dacians used to rejoice when someone died, as they thought that beyond was to be found happiness. This is a historical Romanian dessert.
And, beware, eat it slowly. Also, choose the right wine sort: some white Târnave Riesling or black Panciu Fetească, depending on the kind of food you have. And, for dessert, a sweet Cotnari wine.
Enjoy!

SWEET BREAD

- **1 kg fine white flour, sifted**
- **12 egg yolks**
- **300 g sugar**
- **250 g butter, melted**
- **150 g raisins**
- **30-40 g baker's yeast**
- **1 teaspoon salt**
- **500 ml fresh milk**
- **1/2 cup Jamaica rum**
- **1/2 teaspoon rum flavouring**
- **1/2 teaspoon vanilla flavouring**
- **1 teaspoon lemon and orange peel, finely grated**
- **1 egg**

Soak raisins in rum, let them soften for about one hour, and then squeeze them. Mix yeast with 1 teaspoon sugar and 2-3 tablespoons milk. Boil 1/2 cup of milk and rapidly blend in 4 tablespoons of flour. Stir thoroughly, until it is really creamy; when lukewarm, blend in the yeast mixture, spread the surface with some flour, and place it in a lukewarm corner, covered with a (paper) towel. Let it grow until it doubles its volume. In a kitchen basin, beat yolks well with the remaining sugar, salt, vanilla, rum flavouring, orange and lemon peel; it must get foamy. Carefully, add the grown up yeast mixture. Work gently with your hand. Gradually, add the remaining flour, and keep working with your opened hand, always in the same direction, from bottom to surface, without squeezing the dough in your fist. From time to time, add melted butter. After all flour and butter are added to the dough, it must be rather soft. Keep working until it does not stick to your hand (about one hour of working). After working, spread the dough surface with flour, and let it grow again, in warm corner, covered with a towel. Meanwhile, oil 2-3 cake oven trays, and then spread them with flour; tap the tray to eliminate useless flour. When the dough doubles its volume, take a part of it enough to fill half of the tray. Gently put the dough piece on a floured surface, spread raisins. Roll gently or spin the dough, put it in the tray, and then let it grow one more time, until it fills the whole tray. Proceed in the same manner with the remaining dough. Before placing trays into the hot oven, paint the dough surface with beaten eggs and spread sugar. Bake for at least 40 minutes, in medium hot oven.

Tip: when working the dough, you don't have to use all the flour, if you see that the dough becomes hard enough before adding all the flour. Don't forget to always work only in one direction. Don't open the oven door during the first 30 minutes of baking. When taking the sweet bread out of the oven, handle it very carefully, and never place it into a cold or draughty place.

Sweets

WHEAT PORRIDGE

- **500 g husked wheat grains**
- **1.5 l water**
- **100-125 g sugar**
- **300 g walnuts, finely chopped**
- **1 teaspoon fine grated lemon peel**
- **1/2 teaspoon rhum flavouring**
- **1/4 teaspoon ground cinnamon**
- **salt, icing sugar**

In the evening, wash wheat in luke-warm water for several times. Put wheat and water into a non-sticking thick bottom pan and set to boil. Cook at low fire, shaking the pan from time to time to prevent grains sticking to the bottom. When grains are boiled and all the water evaporated, blend in sugar and some salt (1/2 teaspoon). Gently stir with a wooden spoon and let to cook for some more 10-15 minutes, until the grains have "bloomed". Set aside, closely cover all the surface of the porridge with a wet towel, and let it cool over night.

Next morning, remove eventual "peel" on the porridge surface, and then blend in walnuts, lemon peel, cinnamon and rum. Mix ingredients well with your hand. Set on a plate, give the porridge any shape you want (round, rectangular), and then decorate with icing sugar, walnuts, bonbons, grated dark chocolate etc.
Tip: you can finely chop only half of the walnuts (to spread their flavour), the others being more coarsely cut.

PANCAKES

- ▸ **3 eggs, beaten**
- ▸ **400 ml cold milk**
- ▸ **200 g wheat flour, sifted**
- ▸ **1 tablespoon sunflower oil**
- ▸ **50 ml Jamaica rum (or some rum flavouring drops)**
- ▸ **1 teaspoon fine grated lemon and orange peel**
- ▸ **1/2 teaspoon vanilla flavouring**
- ▸ **oil for frying, salt**

Thoroughly blend eggs, rum, vanilla, lemon peel, oil, salt and flour with a mixer. Add milk, little by little, and keep beating. It must be a medium fluid batter, almost like half-and-half. Pour 1.5-2 tablespoons mixture in a well greased hot medium frying pan, spreading the mixture by a turning movement. When it becomes golden and thick, carefully turn the pancake on the other side, with a spatula.

Spread jam on each pancake, then fold or roll. Serve it hot.

Tip: you can also serve these pancake rolls filled with jam and covered with sour cream. Sour cherry or strawberry jams are the best.

PASCA

FOR THE DOUGH:
- **600 g flour, sifted**
- **30 g baker's yeast**
- **7 egg yolks**
- **200 g sugar**
- **150 g butter, melted**
- **150 g raisins**
- **30-40 g**
- **1 teaspoon salt**
- **500 ml fresh milk**
- **1/2 cup Jamaica rum**
- **1/2 teaspoon rum flavouring**
- **1/2 teaspoon vanilla flavouring**
- **1 teaspoon lemon and orange peel, finely grated**
- **1 egg**

FOR THE STUFFING:
- **800 g cottage cheese**
- **200 g sugar**
- **1 tablespoon flour**
- **3-4 eggs, beaten**
- **1 tablespoon semolina**
- **100 g raisins**
- **vanilla sugar or vanilla flavouring**
- **1/2 tablespoon finely grated lemon peel**
- **salt**
- **50 g butter, melted**
- **100 g sour cream**

Pasca – is a traditional, Romanian, Easter cake prepared using cottage cheese. You would be hard pressed to find Romanian people all over the world celebrating Easter without pasca.

Make the dough following the sweet bread recipe. Place more than half of it into a big, round and tall oven tray (or a pan). From the remaining dough make a circle, and place it over the first layer, all around the tray margins. Let it grow in a warm place.

Prepare the stuffing. Blend well cheese, egg yolks, butter, sour cream, sugar, salt, flour, semolina, lemon peel and raisins. Beat egg whites and gently mix them into the cheese mixture. Place the cheese mixture into the hollow of the grown up dough, spread some raisins, paint over with beaten egg. Bake in medium hot oven.

Tip: traditional Easter cake. It can be served lukewarm or cold.

MUCENICI

- **1 kg sweet bread dough**
- **1 egg**
- **500 g honey**
- **500 g walnuts, chopped**
- **powdered sugar, vanilla sugar**

Mucenici are eight shaped figures made out of dough that are a traditional staple used on the day the Romanians celebrate the 40 Martyrs of Sebaste, on the 9th of March. In southern Romania the eight shaped this dessert is smaller and boiled in water containing cinnamon, sugar, and walnuts. In the eastern Moldavian portions of the country the mucenici are bigger and oven baked and no boiling accurse.

Prepare the dough following the instructions for the sweet bread recipe. Make 25-30 cm long finger thick dough rolls. Make an eight shape of each roll. Place eights on oiled and floured oven trays, paint them with beaten egg, and then bake in moderate hot oven for 45 minutes.

Warm the honey, diluted with some 2 tablespoons water. Moist hot baked eights with honey spread over powder sugar and ground walnuts. Tip: tile tree or wild flowers honey is the best choice.

CHEESE DONUTS WITH SOUR CREAM

- ▸ **500 g cottage cheese**
- ▸ **200 g wheat flour, sifted**
- ▸ **2 eggs, beaten**
- ▸ **50 g sugar**
- ▸ **2 g baking soda**
- ▸ **50 g semolina**
- ▸ **oil for deep frying**
- ▸ **salt, vanilla, grated lemon peel**

Thoroughly mix cheese, flour, eggs, sugar, baking soda, lemon peel, vanilla, semolina and salt. Form donuts, with a hole in the middle made with your finger. Deep-fry donuts in hot oil, until golden on both sides.

Spread with some powdered sugar, and serve them hot, with sour cream and jam.

Tip: sour-cherry jam is the best choice.

Recipes Index